I Like - Book 5
VI

By Viola & Zaida Stefano

The rights of Viola & Zaida Stefano to be identified as the authors of this work have been asserted by them in accordance with the **Copyright Amendment (Moral Rights) Act 2000.**

All rights reserved. Apart from any use as permitted by the authors & under the **Copyright Act 1968**, no part may be reproduced, copied, scanned, stored in a retrieval system, recorded, or shared, by any means or in any form, without prior written permission from the publisher.

A catalogue record of this book is available from the **National Library of Australia.**

ISBN: 978-0-6458056-4-2

Authors: Viola Stefano & Zaida Stefano
Illustrations, cover & internal designs: Zaida Stefano

Illustrations copyright © Zaida Stefano 2022
Design copyright © Zaida Stefano 2022

Disclaimer: The content presented in this book is meant for educational purposes only. The authors & publisher claim no accountability to any entity or person for any liability, damage, or loss caused or assumed to be caused directly or indirectly as a consequence of the application, use, or interpretation of the material in this book.

VeeZee Publications

Copyright © VeeZee Publications Pty Ltd 2022
First published in Australia in 2022
by VeeZee Publications Pty Ltd
veezeepublications.com

Learning made easy with

VeeZee!

- Focus Core words in 'I Like - book 5' and the 'I Like' series
- Secondary Core words in 'I Like - book 5' and the 'I Like' series
- Other secondary Core words in the 'I Like' series but **NOT** in 'I Like - book 5'

Core Vocabulary used throughout **VeeZee Publications**				
I	want	can	stop	**look**
like	**more**	**he**	go	see
here	what	**do**	**the**	**and**
out	where	**we**	**it**	**up**
not	**they**	when	**that**	**down**
she	now	them	is	put
help	off	**you**	yes	on
turn	who	**this**	no	why
done	make	a	**to**	under
come	in	some	which	**there**
open	get	good	same	home

Supporting students with low vision (vision impairment - VI)

Our VI range has been especially developed to give children with low vision the very best opportunity to learn. The illustrations in the VI version of the readers, replicate key elements of the photographs included in the other version of the readers. We have done this so that all students engage with the same content. Yellow framing is used around each illustration to support children with low vision to focus on the illustrations more readily. Each book is carefully designed with deliberate and strategic use of colour, background and contrast for typescript and for illustrations. Placing these colours onto a black background supports children with low vision to see the illustrations more successfully because of the contrast provided. Teachers should provide guidance to their students by talking about the colours, lines and themes of each illustration. Ask questions using Core words; who, what, where, when and why, to reinforce their associations with surrounding words. The illustrations with their vibrant colours included in our VI range have been created to promote student interest, engagement and learning. Please ensure that classroom lighting provides optimal conditions for students to engage with the VI readers. We advise that students without a vision impairment also explore the readers designed for students with low vision. This will support interaction and discussion amongst the students. It is our hope that this will ultimately promote acceptance, understanding, compassion and teamwork, thus cultivating true inclusion.

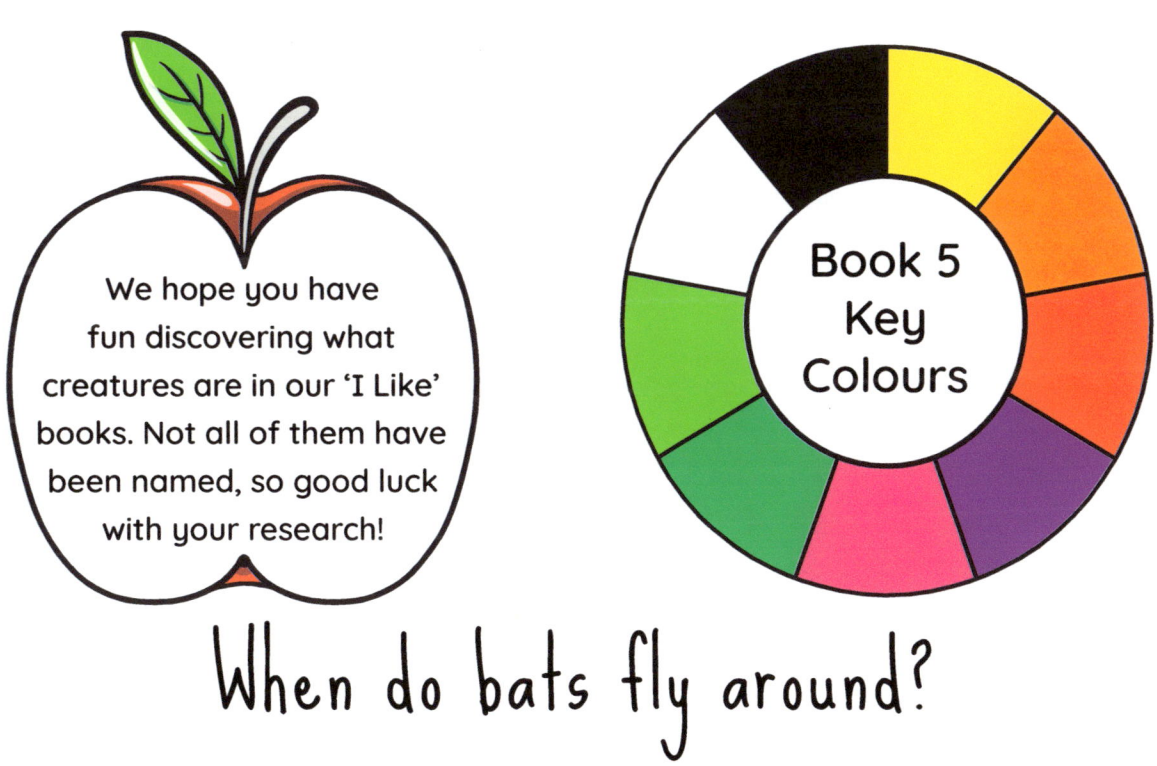

We hope you have fun discovering what creatures are in our 'I Like' books. Not all of them have been named, so good luck with your research!

Book 5 Key Colours

When do bats fly around?

I like to look at it.

You like to look at it.

We like to look at it.

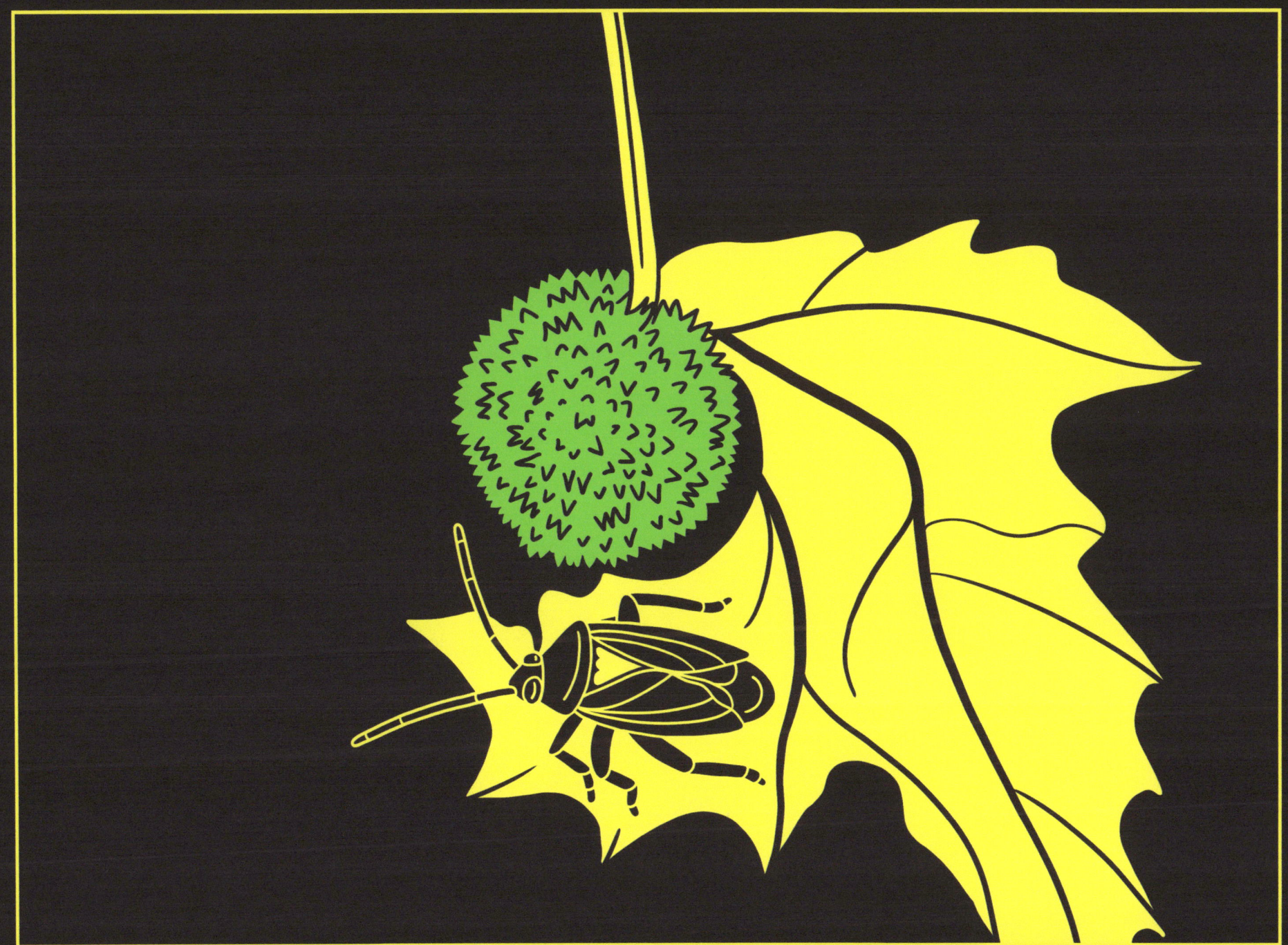

They like to look at it.

Mum and I like to look here.

Dad and I like to look there.

Mum and dad like to look up.

Dad and I like to look down.

Dad and I like that.

You and I like this.

We like that more.

I do not like the spider.

I like to look at this.

He likes to look at this.

She likes to look at that.

I like to look at this more.

I like to look at that too.

Words in this book

I	like	to
too	down	up
here	look	there
they	mum	dad
spider	she	he

Words in this book

at	it	do
this	the	not
that	and	likes
you	more	we

Do you know the focus Core words: 'I' and 'like'? Read the words along each line.

like	I	like	I	like	like	I
I	like	I	like	like	I	like
I	like	I	like	I	like	I
like	I	like	like	like	I	like
I	like	I	like	I	like	I
like	like	I	like	I	like	like
I	like	I	I	like	I	like

Do you know the focus and secondary Core words in this book (refer to Core word table)? Find them along each line, point to them and say them. Read the other words too once you have pointed to the Core words.

I	the	spider	it	we	like	I
he	I	like	mum	I	that	like
I	likes	they	I	dad	like	I
I	look	like	up	at	too	like
like	this	I	there	more	like	do
and	to	like	you	I	down	she
I	like	here	I	not	like	I

How many times did you read the word 'I'? How many times did you read the word 'like'?

Make new words with '__ook', e.g., 'cook'. Write sentences using these words.

Revision: 'I like' Books 1 – 5 - Read along each line.

I like red, yellow, purple and orange.

I like the spider and the ant.

I like bees and I like the flowers.

I like it and you like it.

Mum likes it and dad likes it.

I like tall and you like small.

I like one and you like more.

I like this and you like that.

We like this and they like that.

Revision: 'I like' Books 1 – 5 - Read along each line.

He likes this and she likes that.

Mum likes this and dad likes that.

I like the look of that.

I like to look at it and you like to look at that.

We like to look and they like to look.

I like to look here and you like to look there.

We like to look at it.

I like to look up.

She likes to look down at that.

Revision: 'I like' Books 1 – 5 - Read along each line.

Mum and dad like to look here and there.

I do not like the look of this.

I like to look at this and I like to look at that too.

I	like	here	not	she	more	they
he	do	we	you	this	the	it
that	to	look	and	up	down	there

Fun activity - Match the words to the pictures.

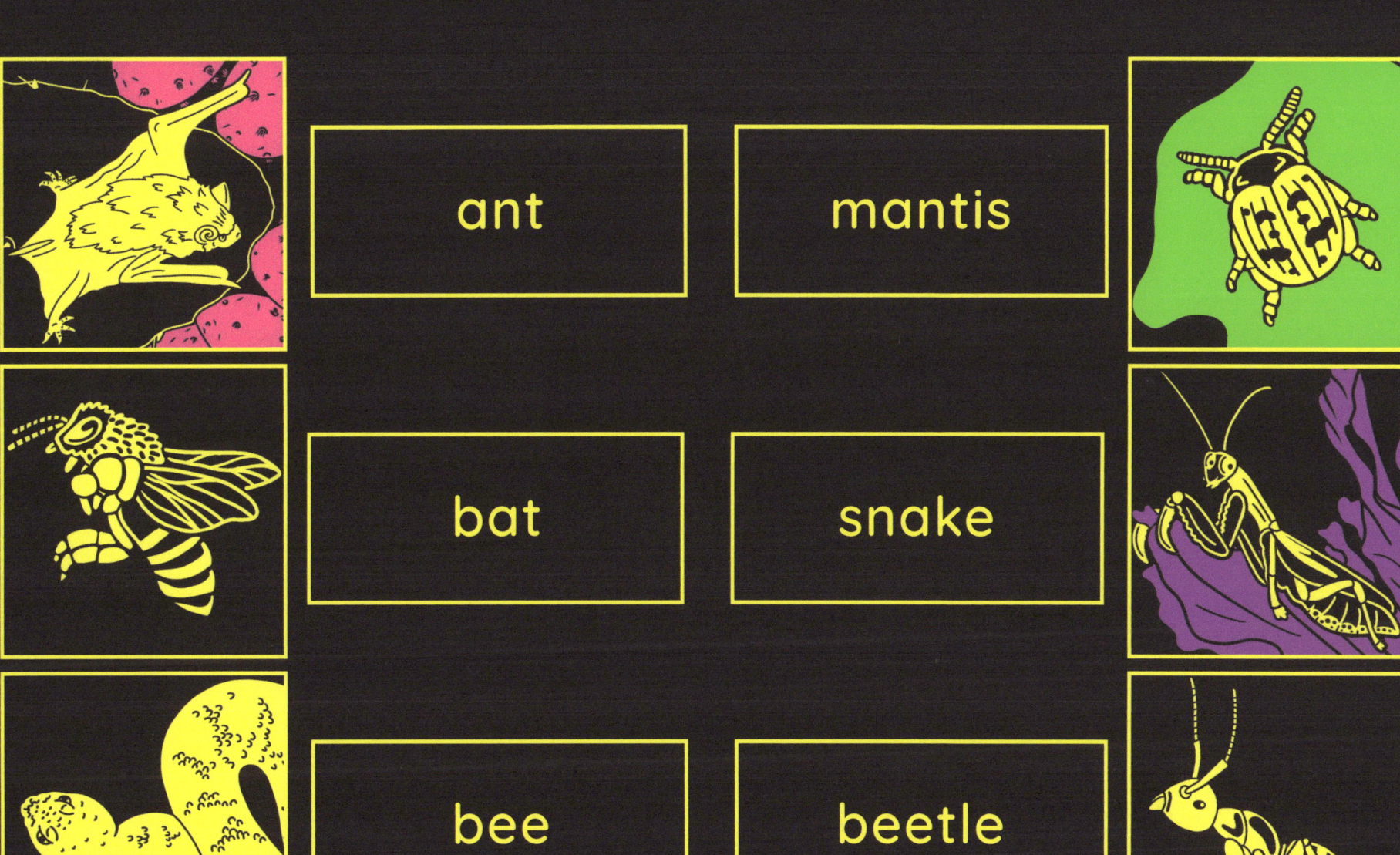

Fun activity - Match the words to the pictures.

43

Fun activity - Match the words to the pictures.

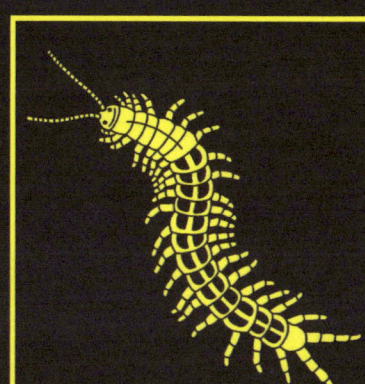

moth

frog

centipede

grasshopper

spider

slug

Fun activity - Match the words to the pictures.

We hope you had fun reading!

VeeZee Publications

Wait, there's more!

Visit our website for information about our range of readers & supporting products.

veezeepublications.com

www.ingramcontent.com/pod-product-compliance
Lightning Source LLC
Chambersburg PA
CBHW040937020526
44107CB00072B/1578